Contents

Words in the glossary appear in **bold** type
the first time they are used in the text.

CHAPTER 1

★

Rules of the Game

It was Dalton's best idea ever. Just before school began, he thought up a game. Three teams would play at once, using a jump rope and two tennis balls. A team could have as few as three kids or as many as ten. The game was really cool. He called it Scramble.

Dalton taught the game to his friends, and soon Mr. Hartel's whole class was playing Scramble. It quickly spread through the school. Kids were playing at recess, before and after school, and on weekends.

Then the problems started. Miss Maclean's class was using fourteen players on a team. Mr. Mancuso wanted to make sure that all students had a chance to play. Miss Ihrig thought Scramble players should wear helmets. The kids in her class wanted to play the game with hockey sticks. A few parents said that Scramble shouldn't be allowed at school.

Something had to be done. Teachers, kids, and parents got together and agreed on some rules.

- Teams playing against each other must have the same number of players.
- Seventeen points would win the game.
- All grades would get equal playing time.
- Each class would elect a Scramble captain.
- A Scramble Council was set up, with one kid from each class. To change any of Scramble's rules, at least three-fourths of the Council had to agree.

All of the rules were written down, and a copy was given to every class. If they wanted to play Scramble, the kids had to agree to follow the rules.

This often happens when people are doing something new. The process doesn't work well unless there are rules for people to follow. It happens with new games, new clubs, and new businesses. Sometimes it happens to a whole country.

The original, handwritten U.S. Constitution is displayed in this special glass case at the National Archives in Washington, D.C. The upright case holds the Declaration of Independence.

★

CHAPTER 2

Plans for Governments

In Scramble, only certain players may jump rope. Players can't carry the tennis balls either. Those are the rules of the game.

Governments have rules, too. The rules say what the government can and cannot do. There are rules about taxes, rules about war, and rules about changing leaders.

World Constitutions

A **constitution** is a written set of rules for a country. It says what the government must do for the people and what the people must do for the government. It may also say what the government cannot do. Today, nearly every nation in the world has a constitution. Some are a single document. Others are a group of several documents. Most of them are alike in several ways:

- Constitutions describe the rights of the people. They also describe the responsibilities of the government.
- Most constitutions say that the citizens will chose a small number of people to represent them. These **representatives** make the laws and carry them out.
- Representatives work for the people. If the people don't like the job representatives are doing, they can elect new ones.
- Constitutions tell how representatives are elected.
- Constitutions usually have rules for courts. The courts must interpret and enforce the laws.
- Most constitutions include rules for changing them.

Balloons fill the sky in front of the U.S. Capitol. They are part of a celebration held in 1987 to mark the two-hundredth birthday of the U.S. Constitution.

GAYANASHAGOWA

Not all sets of laws are written down. Among the Iroquois tribes of New York, the laws were spoken. Older people taught them to younger people. The laws were passed down for more than one hundred years. This set of laws was called Gayanashagowa. That means "the great law of peace." Among its rules were:

- All people are born with rights.
- Leaders serve the people; they don't rule them.
- Each tribe rules itself through a group of chosen leaders.
- Tribal leaders meet to find ways for the tribes to work together.

Early Constitutions

Constitutions have been around for a long time. The Code of Hammurabi has some of the world's oldest written laws. About 4,800 years ago, Hammurabi was the king of Babylonia—the country now called Iraq. His laws included the famous "an eye for an eye; a tooth for a tooth."

Another constitution was written in England in 1215. Landowners and church leaders forced the king to sign a document. It was called the *Magna Carta*. The document said what the king could do—and what he could not do. The *Magna Carta* was a written agreement between the king and the people of England. The people agreed to be ruled by the king, but they controlled his power.

THESE LAWS ROCK

Hammurabi's Code had 282 written laws. They weren't written on paper, however. They were carved into a tall, black stone. The stone still exists. It's in the Louvre Museum in Paris, France.

New Ideas From Europe

Between 1650 and 1750, there were many discoveries in science, math, and medicine. The period is known as the Age of Enlightenment. People began thinking about the world in new ways. In Europe, where most countries were still ruled by kings, some people began thinking about new forms of government.

An English writer named John Locke said that all people were born with rights. The government should protect those rights. If it did not, the people should change the government.

A Frenchman, Baron de Montesquieu, wrote that governments should be divided into parts. That way, no one part of the government would be too powerful.

French writer Jean-Jacques Rousseau said that government was "a social contract" between people and their leaders. Both should make the laws. Laws should not be obeyed if the people did not agree with them.

These ideas made their way to America. They were studied by the **framers** who wrote the U.S. Constitution.

An unhappy King John of England (sitting) was forced to sign the *Magna Carta* in 1215.

★

CHAPTER 3

Creating the U.S. Constitution

Before the rules for Scramble were written down, the game did not go well. Younger kids said older kids should get one less player. Mr. Hartel's class began using baseballs instead of tennis balls. Miss Maclean's kids had co-captains on each team. Each class was making its own rules.

It was much the same when the United States began. The new country did not work very well. Each state was doing its own thing.

This painting shows the signing of the U.S. Constitution in 1787. George Washington stands on the platform.

FATHER OF THE CONSTITUTION

The writers of the Constitution wanted to keep their discussions secret. They had armed guards at the door to keep people out! James Madison took notes about what was said. He kept the notes secret until he died. He was the only framer to attend every meeting, and he played an important part in writing the Constitution. Madison also helped write the first ten **amendments**—the **Bill of Rights**. For his work, Madison is often called the "Father of the Constitution." He later became the fourth president of the United States.

The Articles of Confederation

The first plan for America's national government was called the Articles of Confederation. All thirteen states approved the Articles in 1781. At that time, many Americans did not want a strong national government.

They wanted each state to have a powerful government of its own. But the Articles did not work. They created a weak government that had almost no power. The U.S. government could not collect taxes or pay an army. Each state printed its own money. Something had to be done to solve the problems facing the new nation.

The Constitutional Convention

In May 1787, **delegates** from the states gathered in Philadelphia for a **convention**, or meeting. Among them were Benjamin Franklin of Pennsylvania, James Madison of Virginia, and George Washington, also of Virginia. The meeting was called the Constitutional Convention. Its goal was to discuss ways to change the Articles of Confederation and to plan a new system of government.

Madison and Washington came up with a plan. They said the government should be elected by the people. It should have three parts called branches. The **legislative branch**, called Congress, would make the laws. The **executive branch**, led by the president, would carry out the laws. The **judicial branch** would decide if the laws have been followed.

Arguments soon began about Congress. How would each state be represented? Madison and Washington suggested that each state should have a different number of lawmakers in Congress. The number would depend on the state's population. They were both from Virginia, so their idea became known as the Virginia Plan.

The states with many people liked this idea. States with fewer people did not. Delegates from smaller states wanted each state to have equal power, as they did under the Articles of Confederation. Their idea was called the New Jersey Plan.

After a lot of arguing, a new plan was proposed. It was called the Great Compromise. In a **compromise**, both sides gives up some of their demands to solve their differences.

THREE BRANCHES OF GOVERNMENT

The Constitution divides the government into three parts—the legislative branch, the executive branch, and the judicial branch. The three branches work together, but each has its own job. A system of "checks and balances" keeps any branch from having too much power. For example, the president can approve or reject laws passed by Congress. Congress can still pass a law rejected by the president if two-thirds of the Senate and House agree. The Supreme Court can decide whether a law passed by Congress does or does not follow the rules laid out in the Constitution.

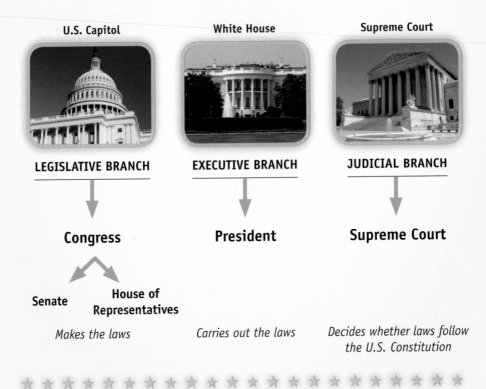

U.S. Capitol

White House

Supreme Court

LEGISLATIVE BRANCH

EXECUTIVE BRANCH

JUDICIAL BRANCH

Congress

President

Supreme Court

Senate   House of Representatives

Makes the laws

Carries out the laws

Decides whether laws follow the U.S. Constitution

The Declaration of Independence, the Articles of Confederation, and the U.S. Constitution were all signed inside Independence Hall, in Philadelphia.

The new plan said Congress would be made up of two houses of lawmakers. One was the **House of Representatives**. States with more people would have more representatives. The other house was the **Senate**. Each state would have two senators. To make a law, both houses would have to agree.

SUPREME AGREEMENT

The United States has thousands and thousands of laws. Very few of them are in the Constitution. All of them, however, must agree with the Constitution. Making sure that they do is the job of the U.S. Supreme Court—the country's highest court.

OATH OF OFFICE

The first election under the new Constitution was held in 1789. George Washington became the first President of the United States. Washington took an **oath**, or promise. It's called the Oath of Office. The oath was written into the Constitution in 1787. It has been taken by every president. It says, *"I do solemnly swear (or affirm) that I will faithfully execute the Office of President of the United States, and will to the best of my Ability, preserve, protect and defend the Constitution of the United States."*

George Washington was the first person to take the Oath of Office as president of the United States. The event took place in New York City on April 30, 1787.

The Articles

When the Constitution was finished, it had seven articles. Each article set rules for the government. The first three articles established the three branches of government.

- **Article I** created Congress as the legislative branch. Congress makes the laws. It is made up of the Senate and the House of Representatives. The article said how members would be elected and how long they could serve. It described the powers and duties of each house.
- **Article II** set up the executive branch. The president of the United States heads this branch. This article described the duties and powers of the president. It said how long the president could serve and how the president would be elected.
- **Article III** set up the judicial branch, the system of courts. The judicial branch is headed by the U.S. Supreme Court.
- **Article IV** described the powers of the states.
- **Article V** set the rules for changing the Constitution.
- **Article VI** stated that the Constitution is the "supreme law of the land." States can make their own laws, but those laws must agree with the U.S. Constitution.
- **Article VII** said how the states would approve the Constitution.

On September 17, 1787, thirty-nine men signed the U.S. Constitution. The famous document explained how our government works. It created the government that we still have today.

Ratifying the Constitution

Before the Constitution could become law, at least nine of the thirteen states had to **ratify**, or approve, it. In December 1787, Delaware became the first state to ratify the Constitution. By June 1788, New Hampshire became the ninth state to accept it. In the end, the Constitution was ratified by all thirteen states. The United States had a new government.

A MORE PERFECT UNION

The men who wrote the Constitution knew they had a promising new country. They wanted the Constitution to make it better. Its very first words—called the **Preamble**—say just what its writers were trying to do: *"We the People of the United States, in Order to form a more perfect Union..."*

CHAPTER 4

★

Amendments

Even though Scramble was a really cool game, some kids thought they might want to change it. That's why the Scramble Council was set up. It had one kid from each class. To change any of Scramble's rules, at least three-fourths of the Council had to agree.

The framers who wrote the U.S. Constitution thought the same way. They believed that, someday, the Constitution would need to be changed. And they were right. Changes were added to the Constitution soon after it was written. And people are still trying to change it today.

Changing the Constitution

The rules for changing the Constitution are in Article V. A change to the Constitution is called an amendment. There are two ways to start an amendment.

1. Two-thirds of the state governments can call for a convention, or meeting. At the convention, states can suggest amendments. This process has never been used.
2. Members of Congress can propose an amendment. Two-thirds of the members of the Senate and the House of Representatives must agree to it. Every amendment to the Constitution started out this way.

Once an amendment is agreed upon by Congress or a convention, it goes to the states. The **legislature** in each state must vote on it. If three-fourths of the states vote yes, the amendment is ratified, or approved. It becomes part of the Constitution.

An amendment can fail because of a deadline. For example, Congress may say the amendment must be ratified within two years. If three-fourths of the states have not approved it by then, it fails.

NO PRESIDENTS

Presidents can suggest amendments, but the president has no official role in the amendment process. The president can neither formally introduce an amendment nor stop a proposal or ratification.

★ ★

THE AMENDMENT PROCESS

The writers of the U.S. Constitution knew the document would need to change with the times. But they built a careful process that would make it hard to change.

1 An amendment is proposed in Congress.

2 The Senate approves the amendment.

3 The House of Representatives approves the amendment.

4 The amendment is approved by 38 states or more.

5 The amendment becomes part of the U.S. Constitution.

★ ★

In August 1963, more than 200,000 people used their right to hold peaceful public meetings. They came to Washington, D.C., seeking equal rights for African Americans. It was there that Martin Luther King, Jr. made his famous "I Have a Dream" speech.

The Bill of Rights

The Constitution described the powers of the states and the U.S. government. It did not describe the rights of the people. Many Americans worried about that. They were afraid that if their rights were not written down, they might be taken away.

James Madison worked to add people's rights to the Constitution. In 1789, he made up a list of rights and gave it to Congress. For months, both houses of Congress argued about Madison's list. At last, both houses agreed on twelve amendments. They were sent to the states.

Two years later, in 1791, ten of the amendments were ratified by the states. They became a part of the Constitution. These first ten amendments are called the Bill of Rights. They protect some of our most important rights.

THE BILL OF RIGHTS: THE FIRST TEN AMENDMENTS

- The **First Amendment** protects freedom of religion, speech, and the press. People have the right to practice any religion they choose—or none at all. People have the right to say what they think. People can publish and read newspapers, magazines, and books that aren't controlled by the government. The amendment also gives people the right to hold peaceful public meetings and demonstrations and to ask the government to make changes to laws.
- The **Second Amendment** gives Americans the right to own firearms.
- The **Third Amendment** says that people don't have to let soldiers live in their homes.
- The **Fourth Amendment** protects people from being searched or having their home searched or their property taken away by the government without a good reason.
- The **Fifth Amendment** gives people accused of a crime the right to fair treatment in court.
- The **Sixth Amendment** guarantees people accused of a crime the right to a fair, speedy, and public trial by jury.
- The **Seventh Amendment** protects the rights of people to a trial by jury in other types of cases.
- The **Eighth Amendment** protects people from being punished in cruel or unusual ways.
- The **Ninth Amendment** protects other rights besides those listed in the Constitution.
- The **Tenth Amendment** protects the powers of the states. States can make their own laws as long as they agree with the Constitution.

More Amendments

The Bill of Rights was among the first changes to the Constitution. But it was not the last. Over the years, seventeen more amendments have been added. The most recent amendment, the Twenty-Seventh, was added in 1992. Here are some of them:

- The **Thirteenth Amendment** (1865) made slavery illegal in the United States. It was ratified soon after the Civil War (1861–1865) ended.

The right to vote is known as **suffrage.** In 1917, this brave woman stood near the White House with a sign that asked the president a question. The answer came three years later, in 1920. Then the Nineteenth Amendment gave women the right to vote.

- The **Fourteenth Amendment** (1868) was passed after the Civil War to protect the rights of all people, including former slaves. The amendment guarantees that states must provide all people equal protection under the law.
- The **Eighteenth Amendment** (1919) made it illegal to make, sell, or transport liquor. This was called prohibition. In 1933, the **Twenty-First Amendment** ended prohibition. This is the only time an amendment has been **repealed**.
- The **Nineteenth Amendment** (1920) gave women the right to vote.

Some Failed Amendments

Not all amendments pass. In 1972, the Equal Rights Amendment (ERA) said that men and women should be equal. It had a deadline for ratification of seven years. Even though this was extended to ten years, not enough states voted for it. The amendment expired in 1982.

Washington, D.C., is not a state, so it has no senators or representatives in Congress. In 1978, an amendment was proposed to change that. It expired, unratified, in 1985.

These women gathered in New York City in August 1980. They marched in support of the Equal Rights Amendment (ERA), but it was not ratified.

★

CHAPTER 5

State Constitutions

During spring recess, Dalton visited his aunt and uncle in Kansas. He taught his cousins to play Scramble. When Dalton went home, his cousins started playing the game on inline skates. Scramble was soon on wheels in the Sunflower State. Even though the rules were the same, the game was different in Kansas.

State constitutions are similar. They must agree with the U.S. Constitution. It is the highest law in the land. But each state has its own ideas about what a government should be and do. And states have a lot of freedom within the Constitution's rules. Like the Scramble players in Kansas, they can follow the rules in different ways.

Former actor Arnold Schwarzenegger became governor of California in 2003. He is sometimes called "the Governator" because of his movie roles as a character called the Terminator.

People in New Hampshire sometimes say their state government is the "most democratic." That's because their state legislature, shown here, has more representatives than any other.

Governors, Legislatures, and Courts

Every state constitution says its government will have three branches. Like the U.S. government, each state has a leader called a **governor**. Each state has a group of lawmakers, and each state has courts. But don't think that all state constitutions are alike!

The governor is the highest official in a state. In New Hampshire, the governor serves a two-year term. But in Texas, California, and other states, the governor serves for four years.

SMALL STATE, BIG GOVERNMENT

New Hampshire has the biggest state legislature, with 424 lawmakers. The next largest is in Pennsylvania. It has 250 members.

CONSTITUTIONAL DOLLARS

In 1968, a large supply of oil was found in Alaska. It was worth billions of dollars. In 1976, Alaska's state constitution was changed. The change guaranteed that money from the oil would be shared among Alaska's people.

In most states, the lawmaking group is called the State Legislature. In Delaware it's called the General Assembly. In New Hampshire, it's called the General Court. Forty-nine state legislatures have two houses, like the U.S. Congress. But the Nebraska legislature has only one house.

State constitutions set rules for courts. Every state has a highest court (like the U.S. Supreme Court) that must decide if laws agree with the state constitution. States have lower-level courts too, and they are all different. In Alaska, for example, there are no town or county courts. All of the courts are run by the state government.

Citizens Take Action

While legislatures usually create laws, the state constitution in some states lets people propose and pass new laws. People write their idea in the form of a petition that gets signed. If they get enough signatures from others supporting the idea, the proposed law can be voted on in an election by the entire state, city, or county. If it passes, the proposal becomes law without going through the legislature.